CASPIAN

ARMENIA

VENICE

ILLYRIA MACEDONIA THRACE

BLACK SEA

ITALIA

ADRIATIC SEA

The Kings of Babylon

NEAPOLIS

MESOPOTAMIA

SICILY

DAMASCUS TIGRIS RIVER

CRETE SYRIA BABYLONIA BABYLON

MEDITERRANEAN SEA
(GREAT SEA)

JERUSALEM

BETHLEHEM

LIBYA EGYPT NILE RIVER SINAI PENINSULA ARABIA

SINAI

RED SEA

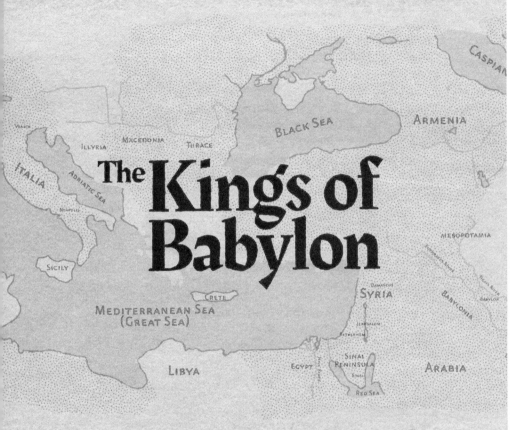

The Kings of Babylon

ROBERT MORRIS

STUDY GUIDE

The Kings of Babylon Study Guide
Copyright © 2020 by Robert Morris

Content taken from sermons delivered in 2019
by Robert Morris at Gateway Church, Southlake, TX.

ISBN: 978-1-949399-98-1
eBook ISBN: 978-1-949399-99-8

We hope you hear from the Holy Spirit and receive God's richest blessings
from this book by Gateway Press. We want to provide the highest quality
resources that take the messages, music, and media of Gateway Church
to the world. For more information on other resources from Gateway
Publishing®, go to gatewaypublishing.com.

Gateway Press, an imprint of Gateway Publishing
700 Blessed Way
Southlake, Texas 76092
gatewaypublishing.com

20 21 22 23 24   5 4 3 2 1

CONTENTS

THE SEDUCTION OF PRIDE

We all struggle with pride sometimes. God has to correct us when we are prideful, but He also restores us when we look to Him for help.

ENGAGE
What is your preferred snack? Do you lean toward sugary or salty?

WATCH
Watch "The Seduction of Pride."
- Look for the three ways Nebuchadnezzar was seduced by pride.
- Consider how God has given us the power to overcome pride.

(If you are not able to watch this teaching on video, read the following. Otherwise, skip to the **Talk** section after viewing.)

READ

The book of Daniel deals with the 70-year period known as the Exile, when God took His people out of the land of Israel and brought them into captivity in the land of Babylon. God was disciplining (or correcting) His children, but He was not punishing them. God doesn't punish us, because He already punished His Son on the cross for our sins. Instead, He disciplines us as a loving Father. God did this for Israel's good. For 490 years, they had not let the land rest every seven years as they were supposed to. The land had missed 70 Sabbaths. If God had not removed the people and allowed the land to rest, Israel could be a barren wasteland today.

When God adjusts things in our lives, Satan looks for ways to attack. There were four Babylonian kings during the time of Israel's captivity, and each king tried to put something of Babylon into God's people. However, God gave Daniel as a leader to all four kings, and as we will see in two famous stories, God protected His people even as He was disciplining them.

The first king was Nebuchadnezzar, and the attack of the enemy that came through him was pride. (Pride was also what caused Lucifer [Satan] to fall and how Adam and Eve were attacked. Lucifer even tried to use pride to attack Jesus). Let's talk about three ways pride tries to seduce us.

Not Giving God the Glory

In Daniel 1:1-2 we read that the Lord *gave* Jehoiakim king of Judah into Nebuchadnezzar's hand. Why? Because God was disciplining His children for their disobedience, and He wanted to let the land rest—for the future good of His children.

Nebuchadnezzar did not give God the glory for this. The definition of pride is not giving God glory for everything you have in your hand. Your ability, skill, intellect, or training did not earn what God has given you. You didn't choose your genetics or your environment. You may have worked to improve things, but everything you have comes from God. Not recognizing this is not giving God the glory. Paul makes this clear in 1 Corinthians 15:10:

> But by the grace of God I am what I am, and his grace toward me was not in vain. On the contrary, I worked harder than any of them, though it was not I, but the grace of God that is with me (ESV).

This is how God used Daniel and his friends to foil the plan of Satan working through Nebuchadnezzar:

> The king instructed Ashpenaz, the master of his eunuchs, to bring some of the children of Israel and some of the king's descendants and some of the nobles, young men in whom *there was* no blemish, but good-looking, gifted in all wisdom, possessing knowledge and quick to understand, who *had* ability to serve in the king's palace, and whom they might teach the language and literature of the Chaldeans (Daniel 1:3-4).

Satan is always trying to teach the next generation a different language and a different literature. Even now, he's changed the meaning of words, and he's trying to tell the next generation that these new words are what our founding fathers meant. The founders of our country meant for us to have freedom *of* religion, not freedom *from* religion.

In verses 6-7 we see where the young men got their names. Daniel was called Belteshazzar, and his friends were given the names Shadrach, Meshach, and Abed-Nego. These were Chaldean names.

Nebuchadnezzar asked his wise men to tell him what his dream was as well as the dream's interpretation. He did not recognize God as the supernatural source of the dream. Nebuchadnezzar actually sent an edict to kill all the wise men because none of them could answer his questions. When they asked Daniel, he said, "Well, my God can."

> The king answered and said to Daniel, whose name *was* Belteshazzar, "Are you able to make known to me the dream which I have seen, and its interpretation?"
> Daniel answered in the presence of the king, and said, "The secret which the king has demanded, the wise *men*, the astrologers, the magicians, and the soothsayers cannot declare to the king. But there is a God in heaven who reveals secrets (Daniel 2:26-28).

What Daniel was saying was, "Only God can do it, but He can use me."

Not Rejecting the Glory of Men

It's okay to honor someone, but only God is to get the glory—and He doesn't share it with anyone.

Daniel interprets the dream, part of which was about a figure of a man. It talked about the future kingdom, and it goes all the way down to the feet of clay. In the last verse of chapter 2, Nebuchadnezzar puts out an edict for all the people of Babylon to worship the God of Daniel. Then we read in Daniel 3:1:

> Nebuchadnezzar the king made an image of gold, whose height was sixty cubits and its width six cubits.

This image was 90 feet high, and most people think it was of Nebuchadnezzar himself. Although he was impressed with Daniel's God, the king required his people to bow down to the image because he still wanted to bring attention to himself.

This happens a lot in Scripture, even in the New Testament. When Paul and Barnabas healed a man crippled since birth, the people spoke of them as if they were gods. Paul and Barnabas tore their clothes (see Acts 14:14-15). Another time, when John prostrated himself before an angel, the angel told him to get up because only God was worthy of worship (see Revelation 22:8-9). Daniel was made ruler of all Babylon under Nebuchadnezzar, but he never became prideful. When God puts us in a position of influence, we are to remain humble.

Daniel's companions Shadrach, Meshach, and Abed-Nego would not bow down to the Nebuchadnezzar's image. This is how the king responded:

> If you do not worship, you shall be cast immediately into the midst of a burning fiery furnace. And who *is* the god who will deliver you from my hands? (Daniel 3:15).

The king didn't thank God for what He put in his hands, and he didn't thank God for the power He'd put in his hands.

> Nebuchadnezzar was full of fury, and the expression on his face changed toward Shadrach, Meshach, and Abed-Nego. He spoke and commanded that they heat the furnace seven times more than it was usually heated ... Then these men were bound in their coats, their trousers, their turbans, and their *other* garments, and were cast into the midst of the burning fiery furnace. Therefore, because the king's command was urgent, and the furnace exceedingly hot, the flame of the fire killed those men who took up Shadrach, Meshach, and Abed-Nego (Daniel 3:19, 21–22).

The fiery furnace was a pit about 20 feet round and 20 feet deep, with a slope on one side to get in and out to clean it and to cast people into it. The fire was heated extra hot by using trees that burned hotter than other trees. It was so hot that the men casting them in at the mouth of the pit were killed.

In verses 24-25 King Nebuchadnezzar saw *four* men walking around in the fire. The fourth person was Jesus. When the king called for them, Shadrach, Meshach, and Abed-Nego walked out of the fire, and even though the ropes binding them were burned off, their clothes did not even smell of smoke. God kept trying to get through to Nebuchadnezzar, even though he was a Chaldean and had tortured and killed some of the Israelite exiles. God keeps trying to get through to all people today too. We talk about how our God is the God of the second chance, but really, He's the God of the second millionth chance! No matter what you've done in your past and no matter how bad you've been, God still loves you. And He is still trying to reach you.

Not Speaking Humbly

A third seduction of pride is not speaking humbly.

In chapter 4, Nebuchadnezzar has another dream, and the dream is that God is going to humble him in 12 months.

At the end of the twelve months he was walking about the royal palace of Babylon. The king spoke, saying, "Is not this great Babylon, that I have built for a royal dwelling by my mighty power and for the honor of my majesty?"

While the word *was still* in the king's mouth, a voice fell from heaven: "King Nebuchadnezzar, to you it is spoken: the kingdom has departed from you! And they shall drive you from men, and your dwelling *shall be* with the beasts of the field. They shall make you

> eat grass like oxen; and seven times shall pass over you, until you
> know that the Most High rules in the kingdom of men, and gives
> it to whomever He chooses. That very hour the word was fulfilled
> concerning Nebuchadnezzar" (Daniel 4:29-33).

God humbled the king by making him crazy. Nebuchadnezzar
became a beast of the field and ate grass for seven years.

It is important to speak humbly. Matthew 12:34 says, "For
out of the abundance of the heart the mouth speaks." The word
abundance is important here. We all say prideful things, but if there
is an *abundance* of prideful statements coming out of your mouth,
that means there is an abundance of pride in your heart. God
always, always humbles those who exalt themselves. If you have a
problem speaking pridefully, then you have a problem with pride in
your heart.

But there is a happy ending to this story. Daniel 4:34-36 says,

> And at the end of the time I, Nebuchadnezzar, lifted my eyes to
> heaven, and my understanding returned to me; and I blessed the
> Most High and praised and honored Him who lives forever:
>
> For His dominion *is* an everlasting dominion,
> And His kingdom *is* from generation to generation.
> All the inhabitants of the earth *are* reputed as nothing;
> He does according to His will in the army of heaven
> And *among* the inhabitants of the earth.

No one can restrain His hand
Or say to Him, "What have You done?"

At the same time my reason returned to me, and for the glory of
my kingdom, my honor and splendor returned to me. My counselors
and nobles resorted to me, I was restored to my kingdom, and
excellent majesty was added to me. And those who walk in pride
He is able to put down.

The moment Nebuchadnezzar turned to God, he was restored to his
kingdom.

God restored prideful Nebuchadnezzar. God restored this
prideful man (me). God can restore you prideful people too. All you
have to do is turn your eyes to heaven.

NOTES

_____

_____

_____

_____

_____

_____

_____

TALK

These questions can be used for group discussion or personal
reflection.

Question 1

What sin sent the children of Israel into bondage? What figures of
darkness wanted to keep them in emotional, mental, and spiritual
bondage?

Didn't let the land rest.

Satan

Question 2

How was Daniel rewarded after interpreting King Nebuchadnezzar's
dream (Daniel 2:48)? Did the king continue to honor Daniel's God
(Daniel 3:1)? What was Nebuchadnezzar's sin (Daniel 3:15)?

Promoted, was given gifts, made him
ruler over Babylon & administrator
over the wise men.

No, the king made an image of gold.
Didn't reject the glory of men but wanted
to bring attention to himself.

Question 3

What happened to those who did not bow down to the image of gold (Daniel 3:19, 21)? How did God protect those who honored Him (Daniel 4:36-37)?

Cast into the fiery furnace.

Saved them in the midst of the fire.

Question 4

Read Daniel 4:29-34. What caused God to remove Nebuchadnezzar from his exalted position? What led to the king's deliverance and restoration?

Not speaking humbly.

His acknowledgment of the God of heaven.

(He blessed, praised & honored Him!)

Question 5

What are the fruits of discipline and correction (Daniel 4:36-37)?

Restoration!

Sound mind, restoration of his kingdom & standing with nobles & counselors. Honor & splendor restored to him.

PRAY

If studying alone, ask the Holy Spirit to reveal the truth about Himself to you. If in a group, take some time to pray for each other as you think about the truths discussed in this session.

EXPLORE

Do you want to go deeper with this teaching? Here are some additional things to think about, pray for, or write about in your journal throughout the next week.

Key Quote

No matter what you've done in your past, no matter how bad you've been, God still loves you. And He is still trying to reach you.

What things from your past might need to be restored by God? How will you let Him reach you?

_____

_____

_____

_____

_____

Key Verses
2 Chronicles 36:20-21; Daniel 2:26-28, 46-48; 3:1
    What truths stand out to you as you read these verses?

_____

_____

_____

    What is the Holy Spirit saying to you through these Scriptures?

_____

_____

_____

Key Question
According to Matthew 12:34, what reveals the true attitude of the heart?

Key Prayer
    Father God, please search my heart and forgive me for any pride residing there. I give You all the glory for what You have done and will do through me. In Jesus' name, Amen.

2

THE STUBBORNNESS OF PRIDE

Stubbornness can lead to our downfall if we don't surrender our will to God. When we submit our will to Him, we proclaim His lordship over our lives.

RECAP

In the previous session, we learned how we can be tempted by pride by not giving God the glory, not rejecting the glory of men, and not speaking humbly. We must learn to humble ourselves and ask God to restore us from any pride in our hearts.

Did you have an opportunity to recognize pride in your life this week? How did you respond?

ENGAGE

What is the one thing you are most stubborn about? (Or are you too stubborn to admit it?)

WATCH

Watch "The Stubbornness of Pride."

- Look for the three reasons King Belshazzar was stubborn and the significance of *see, hear,* and *know.*

> • Watch for the key principle to overcoming stubbornness.
> (If you are not able to watch this teaching on video, read the
> following. Otherwise, skip to the **Talk** section after viewing.)

READ

Belshazzar was the second ruler during the Babylonian Exile. His mother was Nebuchadnezzar's daughter. His father, Nabonidus, was actually the king, but Nabonidus traveled around (primarily in Arabia), erecting altars to the god "Sin." As the Crown Prince, Belshazzar was left to act as king.

For this lesson we will use the whole text of Daniel 5:1–31, which covers the 17-year rule of Belshazzar from 556 to 539 BC.

Belshazzar the king made a great feast for a thousand of his lords, and drank wine in the presence of the thousand. While he tasted the wine, Belshazzar gave the command to bring the gold and silver vessels which his father Nebuchadnezzar had taken from the temple which *had been* in Jerusalem, that the king and his lords, his wives, and his concubines might drink from them. Then they brought the gold vessels that had been taken from the temple of the house of God which *had been* in Jerusalem; and the king and his lords, his wives, and his concubines drank from them. They drank wine, and praised the gods of gold and silver, bronze and iron, wood and stone.

In the same hour the fingers of a man's hand appeared and wrote opposite the lampstand on the plaster of the wall of the king's

palace; and the king saw the part of the hand that wrote. Then
the king's countenance changed, and his thoughts troubled him,
so that the joints of his hips were loosened and his knees knocked
against each other. The king cried aloud to bring in the astrologers,
the Chaldeans, and the soothsayers. The king spoke, saying to the
wise *men* of Babylon, "Whoever reads this writing, and tells me its
interpretation, shall be clothed with purple and *have* a chain of gold
around his neck; and he shall be the third ruler in the kingdom."
Now all the king's wise *men* came, but they could not read the
writing, or make known to the king its interpretation. Then King
Belshazzar was greatly troubled, his countenance was changed, and
his lords were astonished.

The queen, because of the words of the king and his lords,
came to the banquet hall. The queen spoke, saying, "O king,
live forever! Do not let your thoughts trouble you, nor let your
countenance change. There is a man in your kingdom in whom *is*
the Spirit of the Holy God. And in the days of your father, light
and understanding and wisdom, like the wisdom of the gods,
were found in him; and King Nebuchadnezzar your father—your
father the king—made him chief of the magicians, astrologers,
Chaldeans, *and* soothsayers. Inasmuch as an excellent spirit,
knowledge, understanding, interpreting dreams, solving riddles,
and explaining enigmas were found in this Daniel, whom the king
named Belteshazzar, now let Daniel be called, and he will give the
interpretation."

Then Daniel was brought in before the king. The king spoke,
and said to Daniel, "*Are* you that Daniel who is one of the captives

from Judah, whom my father the king brought from Judah? I have heard of you, that the Spirit of God *is* in you, and *that* light and understanding and excellent wisdom are found in you. Now the wise *men,* the astrologers, have been brought in before me, that they should read this writing and make known to me its interpretation, but they could not give the interpretation of the thing. And I have heard of you, that you can give interpretations and explain enigmas. Now if you can read the writing and make known to me its interpretation, you shall be clothed with purple and *have* a chain of gold around your neck, and shall be the third ruler in the kingdom."

Then Daniel answered, and said before the king, "Let your gifts be for yourself, and give your rewards to another; yet I will read the writing to the king, and make known to him the interpretation. O king, the Most High God gave Nebuchadnezzar your father a kingdom and majesty, glory and honor. And because of the majesty that He gave him, all peoples, nations, and languages trembled and feared before him. Whomever he wished, he executed; whomever he wished, he kept alive; whomever he wished, he set up; and whomever he wished, he put down. But when his heart was lifted up, and his spirit was hardened in pride, he was deposed from his kingly throne, and they took his glory from him. Then he was driven from the sons of men, his heart was made like the beasts, and his dwelling *was* with the wild donkeys. They fed him with grass like oxen, and his body was wet with the dew of heaven, till he knew that the Most High God rules in the kingdom of men, and appoints over it whomever He chooses.

"But you his son, Belshazzar, have not humbled your heart, although you knew all this. And you have lifted yourself up against the Lord of heaven. They have brought the vessels of His house before you, and you and your lords, your wives and your concubines, have drunk wine from them. And you have praised the gods of silver and gold, bronze and iron, wood and stone, which do not see or hear or know; and the God who *holds* your breath in His hand and owns all your ways, you have not glorified. Then the fingers of the hand were sent from Him, and this writing was written.

"And this is the inscription that was written:

MENE, MENE, TEKEL, UPHARSIN.

This *is* the interpretation of *each* word. MENE: God has numbered your kingdom, and finished it; TEKEL: You have been weighed in the balances, and found wanting; PERES: Your kingdom has been divided, and given to the Medes and Persians." Then Belshazzar gave the command, and they clothed Daniel with purple and *put* a chain of gold around his neck, and made a proclamation concerning him that he should be the third ruler in the kingdom.

That very night Belshazzar, king of the Chaldeans, was slain. And Darius the Mede received the kingdom, *being* about sixty-two years old.

Belshazzar held a banquet with a thousand of his lords using the gold vessels that his father, Nebuchadnezzar, had taken from the temple. (The term *father* is often used for all patriarchal ancestors). Belshazzar took these temple items and put them to his own use. This was the tipping point with God.

They drank wine and praised the gods of gold and silver, bronze and iron, wood and stone. At that same hour, the fingers of the hand of God appeared and wrote on the wall of the palace. Belshazzar could not read the message. This so distressed the king that his knees knocked. Notice that the king *saw* the hand of God.

The king called and asked the wise men to read the writing and tell what it meant. He offered rewards to anyone who could do so, including making that person third in the kingdom after Belshazzar (remember Nabonidus was actually king).

When the wise men were unable to do so, the queen came and reminded Belshazzar—at some length and in detail—about how Daniel had miraculous wisdom and power to interpret King Nebuchadnezzar's dream. She also mentioned that the king had named Daniel "Belteshazzar."

Note the similarity in names. Bel means 'god,' and Belshazzar means 'protector of the king' (who was considered the main god), as he was protecting the kingdom in Nabonidus' absence. Belteshazzar means 'protector of the king's wife.' See how God has orchestrated this, so that when the queen, who could have been killed because of her impertinence, comes to suggest Daniel, his name is protector of the king's wife.

The king reminded Daniel of his place as a slave (one of the captives of Judah). He said that he had *heard* of Daniel and his wisdom and understanding. He offered the gifts of wealth and power, which Daniel didn't care about receiving. Daniel offered to interpret the writing, but he would be taken care of by God.

You will notice that Daniel later did accept the reward and position. I believe he did this because he realized Belshazzar would be killed, and he wanted the new ruler to know that he had received this appointment of leadership for the purposes of God.

Daniel described what happened to Nebuchadnezzar, explaining that the king was given back his rule when he ultimately gave glory to the true God. But Belshazzar did not humble his heart, even though he *knew* all this.

Daniel rebuked the king for using the vessels to praise the gods of silver and gold, bronze and iron, and wood and stone, which do not *see or hear or know*. Daniel had not been at the banquet, so he could only have known this by divine revelation.

In the original Hebrew language, there were no vowels, and the language was written from right to left. This would have baffled the Chaldeans, but Daniel probably easily understood the writing from God.

MENE, MENE, TEKEL, UPHARSIN.

MN refers to 50 shekels, but it means 'numbered.' TKL is the word for shekel, but it means 'weighed.' U is 'and.' PHRSN refers to a half shekel, but it means 'divided.' Thus in verses 26–28, Daniel gives the interpretation: "MENE: God has numbered your kingdom, and finished it; TEKEL: You have been weighed in the balances, and found wanting; PHARSIN: Your kingdom has been divided, and given to the Medes and Persians." Belshazzar gave Daniel his reward, and that night the king died and was succeeded by Darius the Mede.

Stubbornness comes from pride. Remember the word *Babylon* comes from the word *Babel,* which means 'confusion.' *On* means 'sown,' so *Babylon* means 'confusion was sown.' So here are the three things about Belshazzar that caused his stubbornness.

He *Saw* but He Didn't *Look*

Moses saw the burning bush and turned aside to look. Belshazzar saw how God was at work in his grandfather Nebuchadnezzar. He knew who the true God was but never turned to look and have a personal encounter with God.

We all struggle with things. When God gives a word to me, it is always for us. We all have areas that we're stubborn in. The key to getting over stubbornness is *intimacy* with God and others. Intimacy means: into me, see. In other words, I give you permission to see into me. We would all find horrible-looking things inside each other. But God enables us to overcome them.

He *Heard* but He Didn't *Listen*

Belshazzar's pride was a slap in the face to God. He had heard about Daniel's interpreting of dreams and the rescue of Shadrach, Meshach, and Abed-Nego from the fiery furnace. Yet he drank from God's holy vessels and worshipped all manner of false gods.

He *Knew* but He Didn't *Learn*

The king could have looked into God for himself. He could have listened and not just heard. He had plenty of evidence, so he could have learned from it, but he didn't.

We Can Turn Our Will to the Lord

My definition of stubbornness is, "Your strong will turned toward yourself instead of God." A strong will is not bad if it goes in the right direction. Some of us have believed in Jesus but have never truly been saved because we haven't turned our will toward Him. The good news is that you can turn your will to Him today.

NOTES

_____

_____

_____

_____

_____

_____

_____

_____

_____

TALK

These questions can be used for group discussion or personal reflection:

Question 1
Why do you think King Belshazzar praised the gods of gold and silver, bronze and iron, wood and stone rather than the one true God (Daniel 5:4)?

Did not want to acknowledge the true God. Stubbornness of pride.

Question 2
How did Belshazzar's prideful behavior influence others under his leadership? Is there anyone under your influence (spouse, children, employees, etc.) who has been affected by your pride or stubbornness?

His kingdom fell to the Medes & Persians.

Question 3

Through the writing on the wall, God told Belshazzar his time was up. Why did God use Daniel, rather than one of Belshazzar's "wise" men, to interpret the writing?

Daniel was the "one" who could hear from God. Also, by using Daniel, God received the glory.

Question 4

When Daniel refused Belshazzar's gifts, what point was he trying to make (Daniel 5:17)?

God was his provider.

Question 5

Belshazzar's death—the same night of Daniel's interpretation—
clearly proves God says what He means and means what He says.
The Lord is sovereign and intentional! Reflect on the times
He has revealed His intentions to you as well as your responses.

_____

_____

_____

_____

PRAY

If studying alone, ask the Holy Spirit to reveal the truth about Himself to you. If in a group, take some time to pray for each other as you think about the truths discussed in this session.

EXPLORE

Do you want to go deeper with this teaching? Here are some additional things to think about, pray for, or write about in your journal throughout the next week.

Key Quote
> The key to getting over stubbornness is **intimacy** with God and others.

What is one way you could open up and become more intimate with others?

_____

_____

_____

_____

_____

Key Verses

Daniel 5:1–31

What truths stand out to you as you read these verses?

God is sovereign & He will not be stolen from. He gives chances to people to change but won't force them to.

What is the Holy Spirit saying to you through these Scriptures?

Not enough to see & hear, but you have to know & learn.

Key Question

How can you turn your will toward God? *Intimacy*

Key Prayer

Father, God, thank You for Your love, mercy, and grace, none of which we deserve. Purify our hearts as only You can, Lord God. Strip away all stubbornness so it does not get in the way of Your perfect will. Keep our eyes focused on You rather than our own prideful desires. Help us develop a strong will for You. In Jesus' name, Amen.

3

THE DECEPTION OF PRIDE

Pride is one of the enemy's most effective and deceptive tricks. But don't fall for it! Walk in humility and swallow your pride—or it may swallow you.

RECAP

In the previous session, we learned how pride can lead to stubbornness, which can lead to our downfall. We must submit everything we see, hear, and know to God and be intimate with Him. Did you have an opportunity this week to recognize stubbornness in your life? What was your response?

ENGAGE

Play the "Blind Leads" game. Break off into teams of two—one person is blindfolded, and one is not. The sighted person can either hold the other person's hand or use vocal commands to guide their partner around the room. Make the path as easy or as "bumpy" as you like.

WATCH

Watch "The Deception of Pride."
* Look for the terrible results of pride.
* Watch for the key to walking in humility.

(If you are not able to watch this teaching on video, read the following. Otherwise, skip to the **Talk** section after viewing.)

READ

The Darius mentioned in Daniel 6 is not the same Darius named in Ezra, Nehemiah, Haggai, and Zechariah. The latter is Darius the great, who was a Persian.

We will read from the New Living Translation because it is easier to understand.

Darius the Mede decided to divide the kingdom into 120 provinces, and he appointed a high officer to rule over each province. The king also chose Daniel and two others as administrators to supervise the high officers and protect the king's interests. Daniel soon proved himself more capable than all the other administrators and high officers. Because of Daniel's great ability, the king made plans to place him over the entire empire.

Then the other administrators and high officers began searching for some fault in the way Daniel was handling government affairs, but they couldn't find anything to criticize or condemn. He was faithful, always responsible, and completely trustworthy. So they concluded, "Our only chance of finding grounds for accusing Daniel will be in connection with the rules of his religion."

So the administrators and high officers went to the king and said, "Long live King Darius! We are all in agreement—we administrators, officials, high officers, advisers, and governors—that the king should make a law that will be strictly enforced. Give orders that for the next thirty days any person who prays to anyone, divine or human—except to you, Your Majesty—will be thrown into the den of lions (Daniel 6:1-7 NLT).

Daniel was so highly thought of that not only did Darius make him one of the three highest officials, but the king also planned to promote him to be the leader of them all. Of course, the other officials' statement that they were "all" in agreement was a lie. The only way Satan can take you into bondage is to get you to believe a lie. That's what he did with Darius.

Pride was the original sin by which Satan fell. You are the most like Satan when you walk in pride. You are most like God when you walk in humility. After all, the King of Kings was born in a stable.

Pride Opens the Door to Deception

If Darius hadn't been prideful, he wouldn't have been deceived. The other officials wanted for him to be treated like a god. So we see in verses 8-9 that he signs the law.

There is a root to pride, and that root is insecurity. I believe Darius the Mede was always insecure because he was a Mede. When the Persians and Medes joined together, King Cyrus, whom we read of later, was actually in charge.

In verse 10, Daniel prayed as usual three times a day (see Psalm 55:17) toward Jerusalem (see 1 Kings 8:35.) This was how Daniel kept from going into bondage to pride—he knew the Word of God. That is also why, even though my children got formal education in something other than ministry, I required them to study theology.

Pride Always Brings Regret

Darius tried everything he could to avoid Daniel's punishment. Darius respected Daniel and had appointed him to the highest position in the empire. He was distraught when he sent him to the lion's den. The king refused his usual entertainment and couldn't sleep that night (Daniel 6:18).

When we make decisions based on pride or insecurity, we're going to regret them. Decisions should never be based on pride. They should always be based on principle.

Many times when you have this root of insecurity, you take on opportunities or get involved in situations because of your personal desires, rather than going to God about it.

Pride Causes Spiritual Blindness

The next day Darius himself saw that Daniel was unharmed. Darius was healed of his spiritual blindness and recognized that the God of Daniel was the true God.

We see another story about spiritual blindness in John 9. Jesus heals the blind man by spitting on the ground and rubbing the clay He made onto the man's eyes. The man was brought to the Pharisees, who simply could not bring themselves to believe that Jesus did what He did, especially on the Sabbath. Eventually, they asked the man again how this occurred, and he replied, "I told you already, and you did not listen. Why do you want to hear *it* again? Do you also want to become His disciples?" (John 9:27).

The Pharisees kicked the man out of the temple. Jesus came to find him and said in verse 39, "For judgment I have come into this world, that those who do not see may see, and that those who see may be made blind." Jesus is talking here about spiritual blindness. The key to this teaching is in verses 40-41:

> Then *some* of the Pharisees who were with Him heard these words, and said to Him, "Are we blind also?"
>
> Jesus said to them, "If you were blind, you would have no sin; but now you say, 'We see.' Therefore your sin remains."

What Jesus is saying here is, "If you would just admit you are blind without Me, I would take away your sin. But since you say you can see without Me, your sin remains. Because you are prideful, and will not humble yourselves, I'm not going to forgive you."

The key to forgiveness of sin is to admit you need a Savior. Humble yourself and open your spiritual eyes. You need Jesus.

NOTES

_____

_____

_____

_____

_____

_____

_____

_____

_____

_____

_____

_____

_____

_____

TALK

These questions can be used for group discussion or personal reflection.

Question 1

Why did King Darius' officers and administrators try to find fault in Daniel? What was at the root of their efforts (Daniel 6:1–5)?

Jealousy

Insecurity & pride

Question 2

What caused King Darius to sign the new law into effect so quickly (Daniel 6:6–9)?

Pride & insecurity

Question 3

As king, Darius probably could have changed the law if he wanted to. Why do you think he didn't (Daniel 6:8)?

He didn't want to be put on the

spot.

Question 4

Foolish pride often has a domino effect. Who else was harmed by the actions of King Darius' officers and administrators (Daniel 6:24)?

His accusers, their children & their

wives.

Question 5

Daniel's experience caused the king to have a change of heart, and King Darius' spiritual eyes were "opened." What are some areas where you might be spiritually blinded by pride?

_____

_____

_____

_____

PRAY

If studying alone, ask the Holy Spirit to reveal the truth about Himself to you. If in a group, take some time to pray for each other as you think about the truths discussed in this session.

EXPLORE

Do you want to go deeper with this teaching? Here are some additional things to think about, pray for, or write about in your journal throughout the next week.

Key Quote

Decisions should never be based on pride. They should always be based on principle.

Can you recall a decision that you made based on pride rather than principle? What were the consequences of that decision?

_____

_____

_____

_____

_____

Key Verses

Daniel 6:1-10; John 9:39-41

What truths stand out to you as you read these verses?

v 6:10 " as was this custom "

9:39-41 It is not enough to "see", but
there is a follow through.

What is the Holy Spirit saying to you through these Scriptures?

_____

_____

_____

Key Question

How can you modify your behavior to maintain a more humble attitude?

Key Prayer

Lord, thank You for being patient with us when we are prideful. Soften our hearts and open our eyes to see You, Father, so we can experience You and all Your glory. Let us walk in humility and follow Your will rather than our own. In Jesus' name, Amen.

4

THE REVERSAL OF PRIDE

We can humble ourselves, or God will humble us. Whatever you're going through right now, God will use it for your good.

RECAP

In the previous session, we learned that pride can deceive us. In addition to bringing regret, the main and deadly result of pride is spiritual blindness.

Did you experience an attack this week that could have been caused by pride? If so, how did you respond?

ENGAGE

Would you rather have a "staycation" or vacation during spring break? What is your funniest spring break memory and why?

WATCH

Watch "The Reversal of Pride."

- Look for the ways God cares for His people as they humble themselves or He humbles them.
- Consider some ways God has provided for you or your loved ones.

(If you are not able to watch this teaching on video, read the following. Otherwise, skip to the **Talk** section after viewing.)

READ

Daniel ministered to the four kings of Babylon during the Exile: Nebuchadnezzar, Belshazzar, Darius, and finally, Cyrus (Daniel 1:21). The book of Daniel has 12 chapters, the first six of which are historical. The second six chapters (7-12) are about the visions Daniel received. One thing you should know about Daniel is that this book is one of the most puzzling books to skeptics in the world. Daniel prophesied things with such specificity that people can't explain it. Five hundred years before Jesus was born, Daniel actually prophesied the year the Messiah would began His ministry.

Cyrus is the surprise leader of this series. He represents the *reversal of pride*. Pride can be reversed, and a prideful person can become a humble person. Proverbs 16:18 says, "Pride comes before destruction, / And a haughty spirit before a fall." God humbles people to keep them from being destroyed. Why? Because He loves us! There are three reasons God wants to reverse pride in your life.

God's Plans for You Are for Your Good

Deuteronomy 8:16 says, "Who fed you in the wilderness with manna, which your fathers did not know, that He might humble you and that He might test you, to do you good in the end." You have probably said, "I know God is humbling and testing me right now." Romans 8:28 says that all things work for good for believers.

Daniel said he had studied the book of Jeremiah and that is how he knew the Exile would be 70 years. Just before the Israelites were taken captive, Jeremiah wrote, "Thus says the Lord, the God of Israel: 'Like these good figs, so will I acknowledge those who are carried away captive from Judah, whom I have sent out of this place for *their own* good, into the land of the Chaldeans'" (Jeremiah 24:5). God did this for the good of His people.

Most of us are familiar with Jeremiah 29:11. But look at the context it is used in:

> For thus says the Lord: After seventy years are completed at Babylon, I will visit you and perform My good word toward you, and cause you to return to this place. For I know the thoughts that I think toward you, says the Lord, thoughts of peace and not of evil, to give you a future and a hope (vv. 10–11).

We see confirmation of this in 2 Chronicles 36:22–23.

> Now in the first year of Cyrus king of Persia, that the word of the Lord by the mouth of Jeremiah might be fulfilled, the Lord stirred up the spirit of Cyrus king of Persia, so that he made a proclamation throughout all his kingdom, and also *put it* in writing, saying,
> Thus says Cyrus king of Persia:
> All the kingdoms of the earth the Lord God of heaven has given me. And He has commanded me to build Him a house at Jerusalem which is in Judah. Who *is* among you of all His people? May the Lord his God *be* with him, and let him go up!

These are the last two verses chronologically in the Hebrew Scriptures. Unlike our Christian Old Testament, which has 39 books, the Hebrew Scriptures have 24 books. The first five books are the Torah, the next eight are the Prophets, and the last 11 are called the Writings. The reason for the difference in number is that some of the books in the Hebrew Scriptures are divided into two in the Christian Old Testament (such as 1-2 Samuel, 1-2 Kings, etc.).

Even if God is discipling His people, it is for their good. If you're going through something right now, it's for your good. Just one example is Joseph in the Old Testament. He was thrown into a pit and sold into slavery. How was that good? God was preparing and humbling Joseph so that He could promote him. Joseph needed to be humbled because he had pride in his heart. At 17 years old, he had a dream that his brothers would bow down to him. Then he told his brothers about the dream. Only pride would have made Joseph do that.

God Knows You Before You Know Him

It is believed that as Daniel studied the book of Jeremiah, he also studied the book of Isaiah. Daniel discovered the following passages in Isaiah:

> Thus says the Lord to His anointed,
> To Cyrus, whose right hand I have held—
> To subdue nations before him
> And loose the armor of kings,

To open before him the double doors,
So that the gates will not be shut (Isaiah 45:1).

For Jacob My servant's sake,
And Israel My elect,
I have even called you by your name;
I have named you, though you have not known Me (Isaiah 45:4).

Who says of Cyrus, "*He is* My shepherd,
And he shall perform all My pleasure,
Saying to Jerusalem, 'You shall be built,'
And to the temple, 'Your foundation shall be laid'" (Isaiah 44:28).

It is believed that Daniel showed these verses, which had been written 150 years earlier, to Cyrus.

Here's the amazing thing: God said, "I named you." When Cyrus was born, his grandfather (the king) dreamed his grandson was going to overthrow him. So he ordered the baby to be killed. However, the guard in charge of killing the baby met a shepherd who was burying his stillborn son, and the two men decided to switch babies. The king was satisfied, and the shepherd named his new baby boy "Cyrus." Cyrus was raised by the shepherd for 10 years.

In the tenth year, the king was in such mourning over the supposed death of his grandson that the guard admitted Cyrus was still alive. The king wanted to be reunited with his grandson, so Cyrus was taken from his adoptive parents to live with his grandfather. Years later, the prophetic dream came true, and Cyrus overthrew his grandfather and become the ruler of the land.

When Daniel showed the verses in Isaiah to Cyrus, the king believed God knew him personally and had a plan for him.

God's Plans for You Include Provision

God provided through Cyrus everything Israel needed for the foundation of the temple to be laid and the rebuilding of Jerusalem.

> And whoever is left in any place where he dwells, let the men of his place help him with silver and gold, with goods and livestock, besides the freewill offerings for the house of God which *is* in Jerusalem (Ezra 1:4).

> They also gave money to the masons and the carpenters, and food, drink, and oil to the people of Sidon and Tyre to bring cedar logs from Lebanon to the sea, to Joppa, according to the permission which they had from Cyrus king of Persia (Ezra 3:7).

This is the reversal of pride. When pride gets reversed in your life, you immediately step into God's plan for you, and you also step into God's provision for you. Daniel, Shadrach, Meshach, and Abed-Nego were provided for. When the Israelites were in the wilderness, their clothes and shoes didn't wear out for 40 years. God provides for us supernaturally.

God humbles us, but that's not the ultimate; the ultimate is that you humble yourself. Even when God humbled Nebuchadnezzar, Darius, and Cyrus, they had a choice and humbled themselves. Belshazzar, on the other hand, did *not* humble himself. Here are just a few examples from 2 Chronicles:

> If My people who are called by My name will humble themselves, and pray and seek My face, and turn from their wicked ways, then I will hear from heaven, and will forgive their sin and heal their land (7:14).

Humility comes even before prayer, because the prayer of a prideful heart is not going to go anywhere.

> So the leaders of Israel and the king humbled themselves; and they said, "The Lord *is* righteous" (12:6).

> Then Hezekiah humbled himself (32:26).

> Because your heart was tender, and you humbled yourself (34:27).

The New Testament confirms this:

> Humble yourselves in the sight of the Lord, and He will lift you up (James 4:10).

How do you humble yourself (rather than being humbled?) The best example is the person who humbled Himself the most:

> You must have the same attitude that Christ Jesus had.
>> Though he was God,
>>> he did not think of equality with God
>>> as something to cling to.
>> Instead, he gave up his divine privileges;
>>> he took the humble position of a slave
>>> and was born as a human being.
>> When he appeared in human form,
>>> he humbled himself in obedience to God
>>> and died a criminal's death on a cross
>>> (Philippians 2:5–8 NLT).

One of the definitions for humble is to rank yourself below others. And Philippians 2:3 says, "Let each esteem others better than himself." Not equal—better. I esteem you *higher* than I esteem myself. I take the form of a servant. To do that you must have the same mind as Christ. You do that by renewing your mind with the Word of God. Renew means "make new again." You can make your mind new again with the Bible and think of yourself as lower than other people.

NOTES

_____

_____

_____

_____

_____

_____

_____

_____

_____

_____

_____

_____

_____

_____

_____

_____

_____

_____

_____

TALK

These questions can be used for group discussion or personal reflection.

Question 1

What does having a humble attitude look or sound like to you? What does pride look or sound like to you?

Humble spirit - very attractive

Pride - arrogant, turn off

Question 2

Who is the humblest person you know? Describe this person.

Question 3

Pastor Robert said Jesus is our greatest model of humility. How did Jesus humble Himself and live a lifestyle of humility?

Took on the form of flesh, became obedient to the Father, even to the point of death on the cross & did not think of Himself as equal to God.

Question 4

One definition for "humble" is to rank yourself below others. Do you agree or disagree with this definition? What would this look like in our lives in a practical sense?

Agree

Put the welfare of others above ourselves.

Question 5

What is the difference between a relationship with God based on humility and one based on pride? Does it really matter? Why or why not?

God can't & won't respond to pride. It does matter. James 4:10 says "He will lift you up." Prayers are hindered when mind is pride.

PRAY

If studying alone, ask the Holy Spirit to reveal the truth about Himself to you. If in a group, take some time to pray for each other as you think about the truths discussed in this session.

EXPLORE

Do you want to go deeper with this teaching? Here are some additional things to think about, pray for, or write about in your journal throughout the next week.

Key Quote

> *When pride gets reversed in your life, you immediately step into God's plan for you, and you also step into God's provision for you.*

Have you had an experience where God provided for you after He humbled you?

_____

_____

_____

_____

_____

Key Verses

Daniel 9:2; Jeremiah 24:5; 29:10-11; Ezra 3:7

What truths stand out to you as you read these verses?

Daniel understood by the Word of the Lord.

God's purpose in reversing pride was

for the good of the people.

God's plans for you include provision.

What is the Holy Spirit saying to you through these Scriptures?

He knows more than I do!!

Key Question

How would our lives be different if we lived humbly each day?
What is the Holy Spirit saying to you?

Key Prayer

Heavenly Father, we thank You for the loving heart You have toward us, Your children. Help us cultivate a heart-attitude of humility. Search our hearts and remove anything that doesn't please you. Lead us in a lifestyle of humility as we allow You to make us into vessels of honor for Your glory. In Jesus' name, Amen.

LEADER'S GUIDE

The *Kings of Babylon* Leader's Guide is designed to help you lead your small group or class through *The Kings of Babylon* curriculum. Use this guide along with the curriculum for a life-changing, interactive experience.

BEFORE YOU MEET

- Ask God to prepare the hearts and minds of the people in your group. Ask Him to show you how to encourage each person to integrate the principles all of you discover into your daily lives through group discussion and writing in your journals.
- Preview the video segment for the week.
- Plan how much time you'll give to each portion of your meeting (see the suggested schedule below). In case you're unable to get through all of the activities in the time you have planned, here is a list of the most important questions (from the **Talk** section) for each week.

SUGGESTED SCHEDULE FOR THE GROUP

1. **Engage** and **Recap** (5 Minutes)
2. **Watch** and **Read** (20 Minutes)
3. **Talk** (25 Minutes)
4. **Pray** (10 minutes)

SESSION ONE

Q: What sin sent the children of Israel into bondage? What figures of darkness wanted to keep them in emotional, mental, and spiritual bondage?

Q: How was Daniel rewarded after interpreting King Nebuchadnezzar's dream (Daniel 2:48)? Did the king continue to honor Daniel's God (Daniel 3:1)? What was Nebuchadnezzar's sin (Daniel 3:15)?

SESSION TWO

Q: Why do you think King Belshazzar praised the gods of gold and silver, bronze and iron, wood and stone rather than the one true God (Daniel 5:4)?

Q: Belshazzar's death—the same night of Daniel's interpretation—clearly proves God says what He means and means what He says. He is sovereign and intentional! Reflect on the times He has revealed His intentions to you as well as your responses.

SESSION THREE

Q: Why did King Darius' officers and administrators try to find fault in Daniel? What was at the root of their efforts (Daniel 6:1-5)?

Q: As king, Darius probably could have changed the law if he wanted to. Why do you think he didn't (Daniel 6:8)?

SESSION FOUR

Q: What does having a humble attitude look or sound like to you? What does pride look or sound like to you?

Q: What is the difference between a relationship with God based on humility and one based on pride? Does it really matter? Why or why not?

HOW TO USE THE CURRICULUM

This study has a simple design.

The One Thing

This is a brief statement under each session title that sums up the main point—the key idea—of the session.

Recap

Recap the previous week's session, inviting members to share about any opportunities they have encountered throughout the week that apply what they learned (this doesn't apply to the first week).

Engage

Ask the icebreaker question to help get people talking and feeling comfortable with one another.

Watch

Watch the videos (recommended).

Read
If you're unable to watch the videos, read these sections.

Talk
The questions in these lessons are intentionally open-ended. Use them to help the group members reflect on Scripture and the lesson.

Pray
Ask members to share their concerns and then pray together. Be sensitive to the Holy Spirit and the needs of the group.

Explore
Encourage members to complete the written portion in their books before the next meeting.

KEY TIPS FOR THE LEADER

- Generate participation and discussion.
- Resist the urge to teach. The goal is for great conversation that leads to discovery.
- Ask open-ended questions—questions that can't be answered with "yes" or "no" (e.g., "What do you think about that?" rather than "Do you agree?")
- When a question arises, ask the group for their input instead of answering it yourself before allowing anyone else to respond.
- Be comfortable with silence. If you ask a question and no one responds, rephrase the question and wait for a response. Your primary role is to create an environment where people feel comfortable to be themselves and participate, not to provide the answers to all of their questions.
- Ask the group to pray for each other from week to week, especially about key issues that arise during your group time. This is how you begin to build authentic community and encourage spiritual growth within the group.

KEYS TO A DYNAMIC SMALL GROUP

Relationships

Meaningful, encouraging relationships are the foundation of a dynamic small group. Teaching, discussion, worship, and prayer are important elements of a group meeting, but the depth of each element is often dependent upon the depth of the relationships between members.

Availability

Building a sense of community within your group requires members to prioritize their relationships with one another. This means being available to listen, care for one another, and meet each other's needs.

Mutual Respect

Mutual respect is shown when members value each other's opinions (even when they disagree) and are careful never to put down or embarrass others in the group (including their spouses, who may or may not be present).

Openness

A healthy small group environment encourages sincerity and transparency. Members treat each other with grace in areas of weakness, allowing each other room to grow.

Confidentiality

To develop authenticity and a sense of safety within the group, each member must be able to trust that things discussed within the group will not be shared outside the group.

Shared Responsibility

Group members will share the responsibility of group meetings by using their God-given abilities to serve at each gathering. Some may greet, some may host, some may teach, etc. Ideally, each person should be available to care for others as needed.

Sensitivity

Dynamic small groups are born when the leader consistently seeks and is responsive to the guidance of the Holy Spirit, following His leading throughout the meeting as opposed to sticking to the "agenda." This guidance is especially important during the discussion and ministry time.

Fun!

Dynamic small groups take the time to have fun! Create an atmosphere for fun, and be willing to laugh at yourself every now and then!

ABOUT THE AUTHOR

Robert Morris is the founding lead senior pastor of Gateway Church, a multicampus church in the Dallas/Fort Worth Metroplex. Since it began in 2000, the church has grown to more than 39,000 active members. His television program is aired in over 190 countries, and his radio program, *Worship & the Word with Pastor Robert*, airs on more than 850 radio stations across America. He serves as chancellor of The King's University and is the bestselling author of numerous books, including *The Blessed Life*, *Truly Free*, *Frequency*, and *Beyond Blessed*. Robert and his wife, Debbie, have been married 39 years and are blessed with one married daughter, two married sons, and nine grandchildren.

NOTES

More resources for your small group by Pastor Robert Morris!

Study Guide: 978-1-949399-55-4
DVD: 978-1-949399-52-3

Study Guide: 978-1-945529-55-9
DVD: 978-1-949399-42-4

Study Guide: 978-1-945529-85-6
DVD: 978-1-949399-48-6

Study Guide: 978-1-949399-65-3
DVD: 978-1-949399-66-0

Study Guide: 978-1-94552
DVD: 978-1-949399-49

Study Guide: 978-1-949399-54-7
DVD: 978-1-949399-51-6

Study Guide: 978-0-997429-84-8
DVD: 978-1-949399-46-2

Study Guide: 978-1-945529-88-7
DVD: 978-1-949399-53-0

Study Guide: 978-1-945529-54-2
DVD: 978-1-949399-41-7

Study Guide: 978-1-945529-
DVD: 978-1-949399-50-9

Study Guide: 978-1-945529-56-6
DVD: 978-1-949399-43-1

DVD + Discussion Guide:
978-1-949399-68-4

Study Guide: 978-1-949399-95-0
DVD: 978-1-949399-94-3

Study Guide: 978-1-949399-98-1
DVD: 978-1-949399-97-4

Study Guide: 978-1-95122
DVD: 978-1-951227-0

You can find these resources and others at
www.gatewaypublishing.com